Positive Affirmatic

I AM AN UNSTOPPABLE FORCE OF NATURE

I AM CONFIDENT, STRONG, AND VIBRANT IN ALL THINGS

I WILL ALLOW MYSELF TO EVOLVE AND GET BETTER EVERY DAY.

I CHOOSE TO BE HAPPY NOW AND ALWAYS

I AM ENOUGH AND I LOVE MYSELF FOR WHO I AM

MY CHALLENGES DO NOT DEFINE ME. THEY DRIVE ME.

MY ABILITY TO CONQUER CHALLENGES IS LIMITLESS.

MY PAST IS NOT A REFLECTION OF MY FUTURE AND IT DOES NOT DEFINE ME.

I FEED MY SPIRIT, TRAIN MY BODY AND STAY FOCUSED. IT'S MY TIME!

I AM MY LIGHT!

I AM RESILIENT AND CAN GET THROUGH ANYTHING! I AM UNSTOPPABLE!

MY SOUL RADIATES FROM INSIDE OUT. I AM BEAUTIFULLY MADE.

I AM SUPERIOR TO NEGATIVE THOUGHTS AND POOR ACTIONS.

I HAVE A MEANING AND INSPIRING LIFE!

I AM WORTHY OF LOVE!

LIFE IS A GIFT AND I APPRECIATE ALL I HAVE.

MY CONTRIBUTIONS TO THE WORLD ARE VALUABLE.

I AM PEACEFUL AND WHOLE.

I NOURISH MYSELF WITH KIND WORDS AND TASTY FOODS.

I AM ON THE PATH TO BECOMING THE BEST
VERSION OF MYSELF.

I'VE GOT THE ABILITY TO RECLAIM MY POWER

I AM BEAUTIFUL INSIDE AND OUT.

I TRUST THAT EVERYTHING WILL WORK WELL
FOR ME.

MY SPACE AND BOUNDARIES ARE IMPORTANT

I AM A MAGNET. I ATTRACT POSITIVITY!

I AM A PRIORITY AND NOT AN OPTION!

I GROW, I GLOW.

GREAT THINGS ALWAYS COME MY WAY

I THINK ABUNDANCE NOT SCARCITY!

I AM COMMITTED TO ALL POSSIBILITIES THAT
LEADS TO A GREATER PURPOSE.

I LOVE THE SKIN I AM IN. BLACK AND RADIANT.

I AM HEALTHY AND STRONG

I HAVE A BRIGHT FUTURE.

I KNOW I CAN BE SUCCESSFUL AND STILL ROOT
FOR MY PEERS

I WILL NOT SETTLE FOR LESS THAN THE BEST!

BEING ME IS HOW I WIN

MY FEELINGS ARE VALID AND I HONOR THEM
ALL

I AM MAGIC!

BY SHINNING MY LIGHT, I HELP OTHERS SHINE
THEIRS TOO

I CREATE SPACE FOR PEOPLE TO SHOW UP FOR
ME

I ATTRACT GENUINE FRIENDSHIP WITH PEOPLE
WHO WANT THE BEST FOR ME.

I INHALE MY DREAMS, I EXHALE MY FEARS

I FIND PEACE ALL ROUND

I AM FOCUSED TO ACHIEVE MY DREAMS.

My greatest glow-up is from within

I honor my commitment to take care of myself.

Rest is a top priority for me

I am blessed with unique talents

The happier I am, the more beautiful I become

I look fantastic in any outfit I wear

I smile and laugh always

My imperfection makes me unique

I am blessed with natural beauty

I am proud of my curly hair

I choose to love and accept myself for who I am

I AM FULL OF LOVING AND KIND THOUGHTS

I AM CONFIDENT IN MY ABILITY TO MAKE POSITIVE CHOICES

I AM WORTHY OF THE LIFE I SAY I WANT

MY NATURAL BEAUTY SHINES THROUGH

I LOOK AND FEEL LIKE A GODDESS

BEAUTY RADIATES THROUGH EVERY PART OF MY BODY

MY EYES SPARKLES LIKE STARS IN THE NIGHT SKY.

MY LIPS GIVES ME A BEAUTIFUL SMILE

I AM WORTHY TO ATTRACT GREAT THINGS IN MY LIFE.

I BECOME EVEN MORE BEAUTIFUL WITH MY POSITIVE APPROACH TO LIFE

I AM BOLD, BRILLIANT AND BRILLIANT.

I ACCEPT MYSELF UNCONDITIONALLY

I ACHIEVE MY GOALS EASILY AND QUICKLY

I AM CONFIDENT IN MYSELF AND MY UNIQUENESS

ABUNDANCE IS MY REALITY

I AM MORE THAN MY ANXIETY

I BELIEVE IN MYSELF

I AM TALENTED

I AM FEARLESS AND POWERFUL

I AM A PRICELESS GEM

I AM COURAGEOUS

I AM RICH IN ALL AREAS OF MY LIFE

I ATTRACT OPPORTUNITIES, SUCCESS, ABUNDANCE AND WEALTH

THERE IS NOTHING I CAN'T DO

I KNOW GOOD THINGS WILL CONTINUE TO HAPPEN IN MY LIFE.

I FOCUS ON POSITIVITY FOR A BETTER ME

I AM WISE AND HUMBLE

I AM TRULY A BEAUTIFUL SOUL

I AM RESPECTFUL AND COMPLETELY SELF-AWARE

I AM A LEADER

I DESERVE THE BEST AND I ACCEPT THE BEST

I POSSESS THE QUALITIES NEEDED TO BE EXTREMELY SUCCESSFUL.

EVERYTHING THAT IS HAPPENING NOW IS HAPPENING FOR MY ULTIMATE GOOD

I TRUST MY INNER GUIDANCE.

MY ANXIETY DOESN'T DEFINE ME

I EMBRACE NEW OPPORTUNITIES

I AM HEAVEN ON EARTH.

I AM WONDERFUL AND LOVABLE

THE POSITIVITY IN MY HEART REFLECTS ON MY FACE

I AM BEAUTIFUL NO MATTER WHAT THEY SAY.

I AM BEAUTIFUL INSIDE OUT.

MY BEAUTY IS WORTH SEEING AND APPRECIATING.

EVERY DAY, I WAKE UP WITH MY BEAUTY ENHANCED.

I AM GORGEOUS, EVEN WITH MY IMPERFECTIONS

I AM PROUD OF MYSELF.

EVERY DAY I BECOME A BETTER VERSION OF MYSELF.

I AM SOPHISTICATED AND POLITE.

I AM A POWERFUL WOMAN.

I AM A PERFECT WOMAN.

I HAVE A GREAT SENSE OF STYLE.

MY SMILE EMPHASIZES MY BEAUTY.

I HAVE COMPLETE FAITH IN MY DECISIONS AND
TRUST IN ALL MY ACTIONS.

I AM FREE OF NEGATIVE THOUGHTS AND
REPLACE THEM WITH POSITIVE BELIEFS.

PEOPLE ARE AMAZED BY MY BEAUTIFUL
PERSONALITY.

EVERYONE ONES TO BE A PART OF MY LIFE
BECAUSE OF MY BEAUTIFUL SOUL.

I AM THE CREATOR OF MY HAPPINESS

BEING MY AUTHENTIC SELF IS WHAT MAKES ME
ESPECIALLY BEAUTIFUL AND ATTRACTS LOVE
AND SUCCESS TO ME.

ALL I NEED IS ALREADY WITHIN ME.

My body is healthy. My mind is brilliant.
My soul is tranquil

I love my skin and I am grateful for its clarity

I feel happy and smile a lot

My genuine beautiful smile warms even cold hearts

I have unique beautiful eyes

I breathe in relaxation, I breathe out tension

I am a positive being, aware of my potential

I radiate confident and enthusiasm

I combine femininity and intelligence beautifully

I have a sweet and melodious voice which everyone loves.

I WALK GRACEFULLY AND CARRY MYSELF
ELEGANTLY

MY INNER BEAUTY SHINES BRIGHTLY

I CHOOSE TO MAKE MY CURSES MY BLESSINGS

I AM A MASTERPIECE

MY HAIR IS THE CROWN THAT ADORNS MY BODY

MY HAIR IS FABULOUS, WHETHER IT IS SHORT,
MEDIUM OR LONG LENGTH

I EMBRACE AGING

BLEMISHES ARE TEMPORARY AND MY SKIN WILL
HEAL WITH TIME

I APPRECIATE MY STRETCH MARKS

I LOVE HOW I LOOK WITHOUT MAKEUP

I AM A BEAUTIFUL SOUL IN A BEAUTIFUL BODY

MY BEAUTY IS INFINITE

I DO NOT COMPARE THE WAY THAT I LOOK TO
ANYONE ELSE

My opinion of myself is the one that counts

I feel feminine

I get more and more beautiful with each year passing

I am satisfied with how I look

My beauty is worthy of celebration

I am imperfectly perfect

I am at peace with my past

I am worthy of good things

No matter what goes on today, I know the truth that I am a radiant powerful and free woman

I am beautiful and worthy of every beautiful thing in this world

I am cultured and smart, yet able to stay humble.

I AM A POWERFUL CREATOR, AND I CREATE THE
LIFE THAT I WANT STARTING TODAY

EVERY MORNING I AM RENEWED AND ENERGIZED
BY THE LORD'S ABIDING LOVE

I AM CAPABLE OF SO MUCH

TODAY IS MY DAY.

I AM VALUABLE JUST BECAUSE AM ME.

I AM IMPORTANT AND MY PRESENCE IS
IMPORTANT TO OTHERS.

I DO NOT HAVE TO BE PERFECT TO BE LOVED OR
ACCEPTED.

I AM KIND, PASSIONATE AND I FEEL LOVE FOR
OTHERS.

I RESPECT MYSELF AND I DO NOT HAVE TO
COMPROMISE MY MORALS FOR ANYONE

I SHOULD NOT COMPARE MYSELF TO OTHERS, I
AM MY OWN PERSON.

I AM BEAUTIFUL AND PERFECT THE WAY I AM, NO ONE CAN TELL ME OTHERWISE.

I AM AN IMPORTANT PART OF MY FAMILY, I AM NEEDED.

I BELONG AND I AM LOVED FOR EXACTLY WHO I AM.

I AM A GOOD FRIEND.

IT IS OK TO BE DIFFERENT THAN MY FRIENDS.

I DO NOT HAVE TO FIT IN TO BELONG OR TO BE IMPORTANT.

I SHOULD BE ACCEPTED FOR THE PERSON THAT I AM.

I CAN, AND WILL REACH MY GOALS.

I AM DETERMINED AND HAVE THE ABILITY TO SUCCEED.

I AM SMART AND OPEN TO LEARNING.

I work hard and am ready to be challenged to get what I want.

It is a good thing to stand up for myself.

I respect other people, even when we have a difference of opinions.

I have the courage to share my true thoughts and feelings.

My voice, my opinion, and my truth matter and should be heard.

It is ok to ask for help when you need it, you do not have to be an island and do everything alone.

I have family and friends that support me and will help me overcome challenges.

I can handle anything that comes my way.

I am strong and healthy.

I AM A BEAUTIFUL GIRL JUST THE WAY I AM.

I NOURISH MY BODY SO THAT I CAN BE HEALTHY.

I MAKE CHOICES THAT HONOR MY BODY.

I AM BEAUTIFUL ON THE INSIDE AND OUTSIDE.

I ONLY SPEAK POSITIVE TRUTHS ABOUT MY BODY.

I AM GRATEFUL FOR MY FAMILY.

I AM THANKFUL FOR MY FRIENDS.

I AM GRATEFUL FOR THIS LIFE I HAVE BEEN GIVEN.

EVEN WHEN TIMES ARE DIFFICULT, I AM THANKFUL THAT I CAN GET THROUGH IT!

I WAS GIVEN THIS LIFE FOR A REASON.

I CHOOSE TO FOCUS ON THE GOOD EVEN WHEN TIMES ARE TOUGH.

THERE IS ALWAYS SOMETHING TO BE THANKFUL FOR.

I AM RESPONSIBLE FOR MY HAPPINESS.

I AM DOING THE BEST I CAN, I DO NOT NEED TO BE PERFECT.

I CAN MAKE ALL OF MY GOALS IF I SET MY MIND TO IT.

LIFE IS NOT ALWAYS EASY BUT CHALLENGES MAKE ME STRONGER

I HAVE AN EXCITING FUTURE AHEAD OF ME.

I CAN REACH ALL OF MY GOALS IF I SET MY MIND TO IT.

I LOOK FORWARD TO WHAT MY LIFE HOLDS AHEAD OF ME!

THERE WILL BE A LOT OF GOOD TIMES IN MY FUTURE.

I WILL NOT GIVE UP ON MY GOALS EVEN WHEN THINGS GET TOUGH.

CONFIDENCE IS MY NATURAL STATE .

My charm is universal

Every decision I make I'm closer to my goals

I trust my gut

I take full responsibility for my decisions

I am in charge of my life

I will do what's in my best interest

I trust in my ability to decide

I choose happy and awesome life

My life is filled with the right decisions

I will listen to my heart

I am happy where I am in my life right now.

I am open and honest with my feelings. I can clearly express to others when I feel hurt.

I AM WILLING TO ACCEPT HELP WHEN OFFERED.
I AM WILLING TO ASK FOR WHAT I NEED.
LEARNING ABOUT MYSELF IS A FRUITFUL
ADVENTURE. I LOVE WHO I AM.
I KNOW MY VALUES AND WHY I HOLD THEM. I
CHALLENGE MYSELF TO QUESTION MY BELIEFS.
I AM CAPABLE OF CHANGING MY MIND WHEN
PRESENTED WITH NEW INFORMATION. THERE IS
NO SHAME IN LEARNING BETTER.
NOTHING CAN STOP ME FROM ACHIEVING MY
DREAMS.
I AM EMPOWERED TO BE THE BEST VERSION OF
MYSELF.
I AM A GOOD AND CARING FRIEND. I DESERVE
FRIENDS THAT TREAT ME WITH EQUAL LOVE AND
KINDNESS.

I AM A GOOD AND CARING FRIEND. I DESERVE FRIENDS THAT TREAT ME WITH EQUAL LOVE AND KINDNESS.

I RISE ABOVE GOSSIP AND TALKING RUDELY ABOUT OTHERS.

I AM EMPOWERED TO SHUT DOWN CONVERSATIONS I AM UNCOMFORTABLE WITH OR THAT MAY HURT OTHER PEOPLE.

IT'S OKAY TO ADMIT WHEN I AM WRONG AND TO ASK FOR FORGIVENESS.

JUST BECAUSE I HAVEN'T REACHED MY DESTINATION DOESN'T MEAN THAT I AM LOST. I AM ON AN ADVENTURE TO DISCOVER MYSELF.

I WON'T LET OBSTACLES STOP ME FROM GOING AFTER WHAT I WANT.

I DID THE BEST THAT I COULD AT THE MOMENT. THINGS WILL GET BETTER.

I AM EXCITED TO TAKE IN NEW EXPERIENCES AND GAIN KNOWLEDGE.

I RELEASE MY WORRIES. MY MIND IS CALM.

LANGUAGE IS POWERFUL. I CHOOSE THE WORDS I SAY CAREFULLY.

I CHANNEL MY ANGER INTO HEALTHY OUTLETS. MY ANGER CAN BE USEFUL.

NEW IDEAS FLOW THROUGH ME. MY CREATIVITY IS ABLAZE.

MY SELF-CONFIDENCE INSPIRES OTHERS.

MY BEAUTY IS UNIQUE. NO ONE ELSE IS LIKE ME.

MY FRIENDS ARE MY BIGGEST SUPPORTERS. I AM A CHAMPION OF MY FRIENDS.

I CAN CHANGE THE WORLD.

I AM MORE THAN THE SUM OF YOUR PAST MISTAKES

I DESERVE SUCCESS IN ALL AREAS OF MY LIFE

I ATTRACT KINDNESS FROM THE WORLD

I LEARN TO TRUST MY INSTINCT

I ACCEPT WHO I AM.

I MATTER.

I AM CAPABLE OF REACHING MY GOALS.

I ACCEPT MYSELF UNCONDITIONALLY.

I MAKE TIME TO CARE FOR MYSELF.

I GIVE MYSELF ROOM TO GROW.

MY LIFE IS A GIFT.

I AM RELAXED AND AT PEACE.

I AM WELL-RESTED AND FULL OF ENERGY.

IT'S OKAY FOR ME TO HAVE FUN.

I WILL TURN NEGATIVE THOUGHTS INTO
POSITIVE ONES.

I WILL TRY NEW THINGS.

I AM SAFE.

I WILL FIND THE GOOD IN ALL THINGS.

I AM THANKFUL THE LOVE IN MY LIFE.

I AM ON THE RIGHT PATH FOR ME.

I AM FOCUSING ON THE POSITIVE TODAY.

I WILL SAY WHEN I WANT TO.

I HAVE THE POWER TO THRIVE.

I GIVE UP THE HABIT OF CRITICIZING MYSELF.

I DO NOT NEED TO BE FIXED.

MY GOALS ARE ACHIEVABLE.

I MAKE TIME FOR MY FRIENDS.

TODAY I WILL LEARN AND GROW.

I CAN DO ALL THINGS.

THE UNIVERSE IS LOOKING OUT FOR ME.

I KNOW WHAT'S BEST FOR ME.

I RELEASE THE PAST AND LIVE FULLY IN THE
PRESENT MOMENT.

I ONLY SPEND TIME WITH PEOPLE WHO BRING
ME JOY.

I AM BALANCED.

I AM GRATEFUL FOR WHAT I CAN DO.

I AM NOT A FAILURE.

I RESPECT MY OWN BOUNDARIES.

I AM MY GREATEST ALLY.

MY LIFE IS EXACTLY WHERE IT SHOULD BE RIGHT NOW.

I EMBRACE MY UNIQUE INDIVIDUALITY.

I CHOOSE TO BE THANKFUL.

I PRIORITIZE MYSELF.

I'VE GOT THIS.

WITH EVERY BREATH OUT, I RELEASE STRESS IN MY BODY.

I DON'T COMPARE MYSELF TO OTHERS.

I RADIATE CONFIDENCE.

I ADD VALUE TO THE WORLD.

I FIND JOY IN THE LITTLE THINGS
EVERYWHERE.

I AM A WORK OF ART.

I CHOOSE TO FEEL BLESSED.

THERE ARE NO LIMITS TO WHAT I CAN ACHIEVE
IN MY LIFE.

I TAKE A FEW MINUTES TO RELAX EACH DAY.

I PRACTICE PROGRESS, NOT PERFECTION.

MY HARD WORK WILL PAY OFF.

I AM NOT MY MISTAKES OR MY FLAWS.

I DON'T LET OTHERS' THOUGHTS OR JUDGMENTS
AFFECT ME.

I AM ADVENTUROUS, FEARLESS AND FIERCE.

I ASK FOR SUPPORT WHEN I NEED IT.

I DEFLECT NEGATIVITY.

TODAY WILL BE A GORGEOUS DAY TO REMEMBER.

I DO SIMPLE THINGS THAT MAKE ME HAPPY.

MY EFFORTS HELP ME SUCCEED.

I CHOOSE TO BE HAPPY.

I WELCOME FINANCIAL ABUNDANCE.

I CAN ACHIEVE ANYTHING I SET MY MIND TO.

I AM KEEPING MY BODY HEALTHY.

I CAN ACHIEVE ANYTHING I SET MY MIND TO.

THE ANSWER IS ALWAYS IN FRONT OF ME, EVEN IF I HAVE NOT YET SEEN IT. AS LONG AS I CONTINUED TO SEARCH I WILL FIND THE ANSWER.

EVERY PROBLEM I EVER FACE WILL HAVE A SOLUTION. THERE HAS NEVER BEEN A QUESTION WITHOUT AN ANSWER. I JUST NEED TO DISCOVER THE ANSWER.

I AM A SMART, CAPABLE, BRILLIANT WOMAN, AND I HAVE EVERYTHING I NEED TO GET THROUGH THIS. WHEN I MAKE IT THROUGH THIS I WILL BE BETTER FOR IT.

I AM SAFE AND I AM WELL. I AM HEALTHY AND I AM LOVED.

I WILL HONOR MY NEED TO REST AND RECHARGE.

I AM COMMITTED TO FINDING 'ME' TIME TODAY.

I EMBRACE MY BEST SELF TODAY.

I CHOOSE TO LIVE IN A WAY THAT WILL BRING PEACE, JOY, AND HAPPINESS TO MYSELF AND OTHERS.

I CHOOSE TO LET GO OF THE OLD. MY NEW PATH IS BEFORE ME. TODAY, MY NEW LIFE BEGINS!

I persevere. I am relentless. I keep going.
I have released all my negative thoughts
and replace them with positive ones.
Today is the beginning of whatever I
want.
I trust that I have the capability to
achieve my goals.
I am worthy of accomplishment, success,
and abundance.
I manifest my full potential to being.
I can powerfully attract what I want.
I move in alignment with my highest self.
I affirm my ability to merge timelines, and
rejoice as everything comes to me with
ease.

The world is filled with endless opportunities for me.

My mind is clear of self-doubt, and I am ready to embrace every challenge that comes my way.

Every challenge I face is an opportunity to grow and improve.

My contributions are unique and meaningful.

It is enough to have done my best.

I am at peace with my body.

All is well in my life. I am immensely blessed.

The universe has my back, always.

Today I am centered in my heart, and closer to God.

My body and mind are in complete alignment with the universe

I will fill my heart with the peace of meditation.

Everywhere I go I attract joy and happiness.

Positive energy nourishes my body, and helps me radiate joy to others.

I commit to living a joyful and happy life.

I choose happiness for this moment, and not pain of my past.

The world deserves my authentic happiness.

I recognize all the blessings in my life, and each of them fills me with joy.

A happy, joyful life is being created for me right now.

My inner strength is invincible.

I have ability to do great things.

I am a valuable person.

I am ready and open to receive good things in my life.

I commit myself entirely to good feelings.

I have a strong will and I can do anything I put my mind to.

My confidence is what drives me the most.

My mind is strong and disciplined.

Courage accompanies me everywhere I go.

I will succeed in achieving my goals.

I attract people who uplift me and believe in me.

I can clearly state my needs.

I WILL BE MY OWN BEST ADVOCATE.

I COMMUNICATE WITH EASE AND CONFIDENCE.

I LOVE MY BODY.

I TRUST THE WISDOM OF MY BODY.

I AM COMFORTABLE IN MY OWN SKIN.

I AM GRATEFUL FOR MY JOURNEY AND ITS LESSON.

I AM IN FULL CONTROL OF MY LIFE.

I AM COMPASSIONATE WITH OTHERS AND MYSELF.

ALL I NEED IS WITHIN ME.

I AM SUCCESSFUL IN EVERYTHING I DO.

I BELIEVE IN MY ABILITIES.

I AM INTELLIGENT AND CAPABLE.

SUCCESS AND ABUNDANCE ARE MY BIRTHRIGHTS.

I am attracting positive people and circumstance into my life.

I am whole and complete.

My voice is important.

What I want is coming to me.

I am creative, powerful, strong, brave and inspired.

I am worthy of compliments I receive.

I have immerse self-worth and inner beauty.

My life is a miracle, and I belong here.

I am empowered to have the things I seek.

Confidence comes naturally to me.

I believe in my ability to express my true self with ease .

My heart is full of gratefulness.

All is well and in perfect condition.

I am safe and secure right where I am.

I am breathing in relaxation.

I am feeling at ease.

I love and accept my body.

I choose to love and accept myself.

My best is good enough.

I have enough, I do enough, I am enough.

I am the greatest.

I spread love everywhere I go.

I embrace the glorious mess that I am.

My potential to succeed is limitless.

I am calm, happy and content.

My life becomes richer as I get older.

I am grateful to be living in this divine female body.

I am at peace with my body.

I CAN POWERFULLY ATTRACT WHAT I WANT.

I AM THE SUNSHINE

I AM SPECIAL, BEAUTY IS MY ATTITUDE

I LET GO OF MY INSECURITIES ABOUT LOOKS

I NURTURE THE RELATIONSHIPS IN MY LIFE
THAT ARE HEALTHY AND SUPPORTIVE AND FILL
ME UP.

I RESPECT MYSELF ENOUGH TO WALK AWAY
FROM ANY TIES DETRIMENTAL TO MY WELL-
BEING.

I APPRECIATE EVERY CELL IN MY BODY.

I AM SURROUNDED BY PEOPLE WHO ENCOURAGE
AND SUPPORT HEALTHY CHOICES.

I BREATHE DEEPLY, EXERCISE REGULARLY, AND
FEED MY NUTRITIOUS BODY FOOD.

I WILL KEEP MY BODY HEALTHY, MENTALLY
BALANCED, AND SOUL VIBRATING.

I MUST RESPECT MY BODY AND KEEP IT IN SHAPE.

I WILL EAT HEALTHY FOR MY OVERALL WELL-BEING.

MY BODY DESERVES WATER IN ABUNDANCE.

I SEND LOVE AND HEALING TO EVERY ORGAN OF MY BODY.

MY BODY IS HEALING, AND I FEEL BETTER EVERY DAY.

I PAY ATTENTION TO WHAT MY BODY NEEDS FOR HEALTH AND VITALITY.

I TAKE CARE OF MY BODY AND EXERCISE EVERY DAY.

I ENJOY EXERCISING AND STRENGTHENING MY MUSCLES.

I CHOOSE HAPPINESS AS I LOVE MY BODY, AND I SUMMON PEACE WITH MY BODY.

I RELEASE STRESS IN MY BODY WITH EVERY EXHALED BREATH.

I SLEEP SOUNDLY AND PEACEFULLY.

I WILL RELAX MY MIND AND STOP THINKING OF UNTRUE STORIES. I WILL ALLOW MY MIND TO UNWIND AND BE AT PEACE."

I AM LOVED MORE THAN I CAN FATHOM.

I HAVE MORE THAN ENOUGH VALUE.

I AM IN CONTROL OF MY EMOTIONS, THOUGHTS, AND ACTIONS.

PEACE IS WITHIN ME, AND I AM HAPPY WHEN I MEDITATE.

I AM COMMITTED AND FOCUSED ON MY MEDITATION.

MY BREATHING IS SLOW. PEACE FLOWS THROUGH MY MIND AND BODY.

I FEEL CALM AND CENTERED EVEN IN HARD
SITUATIONS.

I CAN TAKE DEEP BREATHS.

ALL MY THOUGHTS ARE ALIGNED.

I HANDLE STRESSFUL THINGS WITH WISDOM
AND CLARITY.

I AM STRONGER THAN I WAS YESTERDAY.

I AM CHOSEN AND WANTED.

I AM SO PROUD OF THE WOMAN YOU'VE BECOME.

MY SPIRIT, INNER ENERGY, AND MIND— I TREAT
THEM WITH LOVE.

I CHOOSE TO RELEASE LOVE, HAPPINESS, AND
GRATITUDE INTO THE WORLD TODAY.

LIFE IS PRECIOUS AND BEAUTIFUL, AND I DESIRE
TO FOCUS ON THE POSITIVE.

I WILL NOT COMPARE MYSELF TO ANYONE ELSE
BECAUSE EVERYONE IS ON THEIR JOURNEY.

My journey is unique and distinguished. I will not criticize myself. I will love myself for who I am and what I have become.

I will only compare myself to myself. I know what greatness I can accomplish, and I will only hold myself to that.

I will surround myself with people who love me and care for me.

I will not look at the darkness in the world around me but instead at the light within me.

I am happy with who I am. I am so glad I am in my skin. I am enough, and I do not need to be someone else.

I am superior to negative thoughts and low actions.

I AM WORTHY OF EMPATHY AND COMPASSION.
I AM TRUE, GRACEFUL, AND AUTHENTIC."
I AVOID NEGATIVE SELF-TALK.
I DESERVE RESPECT, LOVE, AND KINDNESS.
I CONTINUE TO CLIMB HIGHER; THERE ARE NO LIMITS TO WHAT I CAN ACHIEVE.
I WILL NOT COMPARE MYSELF TO ANYONE ELSE BECAUSE EVERYONE IS ON THEIR JOURNEY. MY JOURNEY IS UNIQUE AND CANNOT BE COMPARED.
I BELIEVE IN MYSELF, AND I THINK IN MY CHOSEN PATH. I CANNOT SELECT THE OBSTACLES IN MY WAY, BUT I PREFER TO CONTINUE ON MY ALLEY BECAUSE IT LEADS TO MY GOALS.
I AM A POWERHOUSE. I AM INDESTRUCTIBLE.

I EXERCISE MY BODY DAILY WITH EASE AND AM AMAZED AT HOW IT CAN BEND, MOVE, STRETCH, AND POSE.

I ENJOY THE WORK I DO. I KNOW THE WORK I DO WILL HELP THE GREATER GOOD. I WILL ALWAYS STRIVE TO PUT IN MY BEST EVERY DAY, REGARDLESS OF WHAT IS HAPPENING AROUND ME.

I AM A COMPETENT MEMBER OF THE TEAM. I HAVE THE KNOWLEDGE AND SKILLS THAT I NEED RIGHT NOW.

MY BUSINESS DREAMS ARE CONSTANTLY MANIFESTING.

I AM TALENTED, AMBITIOUS, AND MAKING MY DREAMS COME TRUE.

I AM WILLING TO DO THE WORK NEEDED TO ACHIEVE MY DREAMS.

I EXERCISE MY BODY DAILY WITH EASE AND AM AMAZED AT HOW IT CAN BEND, MOVE, STRETCH, AND POSE.

I ENJOY THE WORK I DO. I KNOW THE WORK I DO WILL HELP THE GREATER GOOD. I WILL ALWAYS STRIVE TO PUT IN MY BEST EVERY DAY, REGARDLESS OF WHAT IS HAPPENING AROUND ME.

I AM A COMPETENT MEMBER OF THE TEAM. I HAVE THE KNOWLEDGE AND SKILLS THAT I NEED RIGHT NOW.

MY BUSINESS DREAMS ARE CONSTANTLY MANIFESTING.

I AM TALENTED, AMBITIOUS, AND MAKING MY DREAMS COME TRUE.

I AM WILLING TO DO THE WORK NEEDED TO ACHIEVE MY DREAMS.

I AM OPEN TO CONSTRUCTIVE CRITICISM AND
WELCOME IMPROVEMENT.

THE UNIVERSE IS FILLED WITH ENDLESS
OPPORTUNITIES FOR MY CAREER.

I AM WORTHY OF MY DREAM JOB AND AM
CREATING THE CAREER OF MY DREAMS.

I AM PREPARED TO HANDLE ALL TASKS THAT
COME TO ME."

I BELIEVE IN MY SKILLS AND TALENTS.

I AM ATTRACTING POSITIVE EXPERIENCES INTO
MY LIFE.

I AM A STRONG, CONFIDENT WOMAN WHO
ACCOMPLISHES HER GOALS.

I AM DETERMINED NOT TO BE DEFEATED.

I AM FULL OF ENERGY AND READY TO TACKLE
THE DAY.

I AM WORTHY OF ALL THE GOOD LIFE OFFERS, AND I DESERVE TO BE SUCCESSFUL.

I AM WELL ORGANIZED AND MANAGE MY TIME WITH EXPERT EFFICIENCY.

I AM PASSIONATE ABOUT MY BUSINESS, WHICH SHOWS IN EVERYTHING I DO.

I AM A SMART, CAPABLE, BRILLIANT WOMAN, AND I HAVE EVERYTHING I NEED TO GET THROUGH THIS. WHEN I MAKE IT THROUGH THIS, I WILL BE BETTER FOR IT.

I AM ALIGNED WITH THE ENERGY OF WEALTH AND ABUNDANCE.

I ACKNOWLEDGE THAT I CAN DO ANYTHING.

I AM COURAGEOUS. I AM WILLING TO ACT AND FACE MY FEARS.

I AM FULL OF VITALITY. MY CONFIDENCE, POSITIVE ATTITUDE, AND SELF-BELIEF ARE MY BIGGEST ASSETS TO TAKE ME A STEP CLOSER TO MY SUCCESS.

I FACE CHALLENGING SITUATIONS WITH FAITH, COURAGE, AND CONVICTION.

TODAY I AM PREPARED. I AM READY FOR SUCCESS, LOVE, HAPPINESS, PEACE, JOY, AND ABUNDANCE! I AM READY FOR MY WILDEST DREAMS TO COME TRUE.

I AM THE ARCHITECT OF MY FATE. I CAN ACHIEVE WHAT I HAVE DREAMT FOR MYSELF.

I AM WORTHY, WISE, AND WONDERFUL.

CONFIDENCE COMES NATURALLY TO ME.

MY BODY, MIND, AND SPIRIT ARE POWERFUL AND PROFOUND.

I LET GO OF THE NEGATIVE FEELINGS AND ACCEPTED ALL THAT WAS GOOD."

I FEEL SUPERB, DYNAMIC FUEL. I AM ACTIVE AND ALIVE.

I AM CONFIDENT WITH MY LIFE PLAN AND THE WAY THINGS ARE GOING.

NOBODY BUT ME DECIDES HOW I FEEL.

"I'M IN CHARGE OF MY THOUGHTS, AND I WILL JUDGE MYSELF APPROPRIATELY

I AM ON MY WAY TO EXCELLENCE. I GO THE EXTRA MILE TO MEET PEOPLE WHOM I ESTEEM AND RESPECT. I TAKE ONE STEP FARTHER THAN ANYONE ELSE AROUND ME.

I AM DETERMINED TO SUCCEED AND WILL NOT BACK DOWN. I ENJOY TAKING ACTION WHEN I HAVE A GOAL TO ACHIEVE THE LIFESTYLE I DREAM OF.

I AM CALM WHEN I AM FACED WITH CONFLICT. I CAN BRUSH OFF NEGATIVITY EASILY, AND I CAN AGREE TO DISAGREE. I ENJOY BEING THE BIGGER PERSON AND TAKING THE HIGH ROAD.

I SEE MYSELF REACHING THE HEIGHT OF SUCCESS AS I ENVISION IT AND WORKING HARD EVERY DAY UNTIL I WANT TO BE IN MY CAREER. THE PASSION I HAVE FOR MY WORK ALLOWS ME TO CREATE TRUE VALUE. I AM LUCKY TO HAVE A JOB THAT PROVIDES ME WITH THE FINANCES I NEED TO LIVE A GOOD LIFE.

I WORK UNDULY HARD AND ALWAYS DO MY PERSONAL BEST. I BELIEVE IN MYSELF, AND I KNOW I CAN DO ANYTHING. I DESERVE ALL OF THE POSITIVE THINGS THAT COME MY WAY IN LIFE.

I BRING SOMETHING UNIQUE TO THE TABLE THAT NO ONE ELSE CAN, MAKING ME UNIQUELY VALUABLE TO MY COMPANY.

MY MIND IS FOCUSED, AND I HAVE CLARITY IN ALL I DO AT WORK. I DO NOT SUCCUMB TO DISTRACTIONS.

I AM COURAGEOUS ENOUGH TO FACE AND CONQUER MY FEARS.

I AM SURE IN MY SELF-WORTH.

I HAVE THE SKILLS AND PROFICIENCY TO MAKE THE BEST DECISIONS FOR MY CAREER.

I AM THE BEST AT WHAT I DO. I CREATE OUTSTANDING RESULTS FOR MY ORGANIZATION.

I AM FOCUSED AND PASSIONATE ABOUT MY GOALS AND CAREER.

I am living my life to the fullest.
Others recognize my work for its excellence, and I am proud to call it my own.
I learn from yesterday, live for today, hope for tomorrow.
My black girl power is magic
Life is short, I make the most of it.
I release the past and live fully in the present moment.
I stay calm in frustrating situations.
I forgive myself and others.
I am at peace with my past, present and future.
Compassion and understanding help me to overcome anger and gain peace.

My intuition and inner wisdom guide me in every situation.

I inhale deeply and let peace and happiness fill my mind and body.

I am responsible for my own happiness, so I've got this covered.

I feel wonderfully peaceful and relaxed.

I let go of everything that worries me to make room for peace and happiness.

My mind is at peace and all tension has left my body.

I am able to fall into a deep and relaxing sleep.

I am so relaxed I am ready to fall asleep.

I breathe deeply and close my eyes to find that peaceful sleep is only a few blinks away.

I RELEASE MY MIND OF THOUGHT UNTIL THE MORNING.

I EMBRACE THE PEACE AND QUIET OF THE NIGHT.

I SLEEP SOUNDLY, DEEPLY, AND BEAUTIFULLY INTO THIS NIGHT.

I LET GO OF WORRIES THAT DRAIN MY ENERGY.

I MAKE SMART, CALCULATED PLANS FOR MY FUTURE.

I AM IN COMPLETE CHARGE OF PLANNING FOR MY FUTURE.

I TRUST IN MY ABILITY TO PROVIDE FOR MY FAMILY AND THEIR HAPPINESS.

I FEEL CALMNESS AND CONFIDENCE WASH OVER ME WITH EVERY DEEP BREATH I TAKE

MY LIFE IS FULL OF PROSPERITY.

I AM SURROUNDED BY ABUNDANCE.

I AM MORE AND MORE PROSPEROUS EVERY DAY.

I DESERVE ABUNDANCE AND PROSPERITY.

I SEE ABUNDANCE EVERYWHERE.

I ALWAYS HAVE WHATEVER I NEED.

I INSTANTLY MANIFEST MY DESIRES.

I MANAGE MY MONEY WISELY.

I AM OPEN TO ALL THE WEALTH LIFE HAS TO OFFER.

I AM A MONEY MAGNET, ATTRACTING WEALTH AND ABUNDANCE.

I ATTRACT MONEY EFFORTLESSLY AND EASILY.

I CONTINUOUSLY DISCOVER NEW AVENUES OF INCOME

MY IMPERFECTIONS ARE MY PERFECTION.

MY FRECKLES ARE BEAUTIFUL.

I AM MORE THAN MY SCARS.

My past does not define me.

I am who I choose to be.

I am in control of my thoughts

I am still learning, mistakes are part of the process.

My happiness is my choice.

My potential is limitless.

I am the only one who can define my worth.

I deserve love.

I deserve happiness.

My dreams are mine to reach.

I am more than My insecurities.

My body is perfectly imperfect.

I have something to offer this world.

My intelligence is not defined by my past mistakes.

It's okay to go after my dreams.

I am braver than my fears.

No one's opinion of me matters.

My talents are limitless.

I am strong enough.

My emotions matter.

My feelings are important.

My words matter.

My life is mine to live.

It's okay to choose myself.

Who I become is my choice.

I will not allow my self-worth to be defined by your words.

My failures built me.

I alone hold the power to change my story.

I owe it to myself to conquer my goals.

THIS WORLD NEEDS ME.

EVERYDAY IS A NEW DAY, FILLED WITH
UNLIMITED POSSIBILITIES.

IT'S OKAY TO BEND SO THAT I DO NOT BREAK.

UNLIMITED POTENTIAL LIVES WITHIN ME.

MY TEARS ARE NOT WEAKNESS.

I AM ALLOWED TO SAY NO.

ONLY I CAN CONTROL MY THOUGHTS.

I TRUST MYSELF TO MAKE THE BEST DECISIONS
FOR MYSELF.

I ACCEPT MY FLAWS.

MY FLAWS ARE WHAT MAKES ME UNIQUE.

MY STRETCH MARKS ARE BEAUTIFUL.

I AM BEAUTIFUL WITHOUT MAKEUP.

I AM ALLOWED TO LOVE MYSELF, DESPITE MY
FLAWS.

I WILL NOT FEAR CHANGE, I WILL EMBRACE IT.

FORGIVENESS IS THE BEST GIFT I CAN GIVE MYSELF.

MY WEIGHT IS PERFECT.

MY CLOTHES SIZE DOES NOT DEFINE ME.

SOME RISKS ARE WORTH IT.

MY LIFE IS MINE TO LIVE.

EVEN ON MY WORST DAYS, I AM ENOUGH.

POSITIVITY IS A CHOICE.

MY DREAMS ARE WORTHY OF ACCOMPLISHMENT.

NO ONE NEEDS TO UNDERSTAND MY CHOICES, EXCEPT FOR ME.

MY FAILURES WERE MY STEPPING STONES.

I AM MY PAST, AND THAT'S OKAY.

STARTING OVER DOES NOT MEAN THAT I FAILED.

MY SUCCESS IS DEPENDENT ON ME, AND ME ALONE.

My failures do not overshadow my success.

I alone am enough.

The only person I owe anything to, is me.

Some people will not like me, and it doesn't matter.

Some goodbyes are necessary.

Not every friend is meant to be my friend forever.

Some days will be hard, but I am strong.

I am capable of healing.

My childhood does not define me.

Sometimes healing hurts.

Fear will only hold me back.

My house doesn't have to be spotless.

Some days it's okay to stay in bed.

There are lessons to be learned through my failures.

My worth is dependent on no one but me.

I can handle more than I could ever imagine.

Life is my gift.

My time is valuable.

Time is my most valuable asset.

I do not have to become a mother.

I am more than someone's perspective.

My thoughts matter.

It's okay to be sad.

My emotions are justified.

No one is perfect, and I don't need to be.

Self-Care is important.

It's okay to forgive, and not forget.

Not everyone deserves my forgiveness.

THERE IS NO COMPARISON BETWEEN MYSELF AND OTHERS.

MY BAD DAYS WON'T LAST FOREVER.

I WILL KEEP TRYING EVEN WHEN I'VE LOST HOPE.

I WILL REGRET WHAT I NEVER TRIED TO DO.

SOMETIMES ENDINGS ARE JUST NEW BEGINNINGS.

IT DOESN'T MATTER HOW HARD I FALL, WHAT MATTERS IS MY ABILITY TO STAND BACK UP.

NOTHING IS PERMANENT, NOTHING.

SOMETIMES AGREEING TO DISAGREE IS THE BEST OPTION.

IF MY CHILDREN SEE ME CRY, THAT'S OKAY.

PITY IS A WASTE OF TIME.

NO ONE ELSE NEEDS TO UNDERSTAND MY BELIEFS.

MY PERSPECTIVE IS NOT YOUR BUSINESS.

I AM MORE THAN MY ACCOMPLISHMENTS.

I AM NOT MY PARENTS.

A MINUTE I SPENT WORRYING, IS A MINUTE I WASTED.

LUCK DOESN'T EXIST, IT'S CREATED THROUGH MY EFFORT.

THOUGH MY RESILIENCE MAY BE TESTED, I WILL NOT BREAK.

MY ACNE DOES NOT TAKE AWAY FROM MY BEAUTY.

THE PERSON I'VE BEEN LOOKING FOR IS ME.

THE AMOUNT OF MONEY I MAKE DOES NOT MATTER.

I BELIEVE IN MYSELF, INDEPENDENT OF OTHERS' BELIEF IN ME.

I WILL NEVER BE ABLE TO CHANGE THE PAST, SO
I MIGHT AS WELL ACCEPT IT.
SOMETIMES BAD THINGS WILL HAPPEN, IT'S
HOW I REACT THAT MATTERS.
I AM NO ONE'S PRISONER.
EVERYDAY IS A NEW CHANCE FOR ME TO TRY
AGAIN.
SOMETIMES WALKING AWAY IS THE BEST
CHOICE, I WON'T LOOK BACK.
WHEN I MAKE A CHOICE, I WILL STICK WITH IT.
THE TRUTH IS OFTEN THE MOST PAINFUL THING
TO HEAR, I WON'T FEAR IT, I WILL LEARN FROM
IT.
NEVER DOUBT YOURSELF, ESPECIALLY WHEN
IT'S SOMETHING YOU'VE ALWAYS WANTED.
I WILL REACH FOR THE STARS, BECAUSE MOST
PEOPLE NEVER EVEN MAKE IT TO SPACE.

I AM WILLING TO CHANGE WHENEVER I FEEL IT IS NEEDED.

I AM STRONG ENOUGH TO SURVIVE MY LIFE.

I AM CAPABLE OF SURVIVING, EVEN ON MY WORST DAYS.

MONEY DOES NOT CREATE HAPPINESS, EVEN SOME OF THE RICH ARE MISERABLE.

EVERYONE IS DEALING WITH SOMETHING, EVERYONE, I WILL BE KIND.

COLLEGE IS OVERRATED, I CAN BE SUCCESSFUL WITHOUT A DEGREE.

SOMETIMES I JUST HAVE TO TRUST THE PROCESS.

I AM THE ONLY OBSTACLE THAT STANDS BETWEEN ME AND MY DREAMS.

TIME HAS A WAY OF HEALING, SOMETIMES EVEN WHEN I DON'T WANT IT TO.

There's 8 billion people on the planet, I am not the only one going through this.

Sometimes blessings come in the form of pain.

I will not back down, I will fight for me.

Self-doubt is a facade, meant to hold me back.

Love even when you're scared.

I will never fear the fall.

Breathe.

The climb is more worth it than I could ever imagine.

Everyone is capable of everything, and that includes me.

I will embrace goodbyes, and be grateful for the time I had.

I WILL DO MORE THAN SURVIVE, I WILL LIVE.

STRESS ISN'T WORTH IT.

I WILL TAKE THE SICK DAY.

I WILL USE ALL OF MY VACATION.

I WILL LOVE MY LIFE MORE THAN MY WORK.

I AM CAPABLE OF LEARNING ANYTHING.

I WILL NEVER BE TOO OLD TO LEARN SOMETHING NEW.

AGING IS A GIFT, STOP FIGHTING IT, WE ALL DIE IN THE END.

HAPPINESS IS THE KEY TO FREEDOM.

SOME PEOPLE WILL NEVER UNDERSTAND YOU, AND THAT'S OKAY.

KNOW WHO YOU ARE, BETTER THAN ANYONE ELSE.

CONTROL IS A DISEASE, GIVE IT UP.

NEVER FOCUS ON WHAT'S MISSING, FOCUS ON WHAT YOU HAVE.

DO WHAT YOU ENJOY.

LIFE IS NEVER FAIR, NEVER.

ANYTHING IS POSSIBLE, YOU JUST HAVE TO FIGURE OUT THE PROCESS.

I WILL LOOK AT MY DREAMS EVERY DAY, AND REMIND MYSELF THAT THEY ARE POSSIBLE.

I CONTINUE TO IMPROVE AND GET BETTER EACH AND EVERY DAY.

I FULLY FORGIVE MYSELF FOR ALL OF MY PAST MISTAKES, THOSE MISTAKES HELPED ME TO LEARN AND GROW INTO THE PERSON I HAVE BECOME.

I CAN GET THROUGH THIS, I CAN GET THROUGH ANYTHING.

Today will be a great day, because I choose to be positive.

It's okay that I do not know everything, no one does.

I will always stand up for the people and things that I believe in.

My experiences today will become wonderful memories tomorrow.

I have the power to control all of my thoughts and emotions.

I deserve to make choices that make me happy.

Good things always come, you just have to be patient.

I matter not only to myself, but to those who love me.

My best is enough.

I HAVE THE POWER TO BE CALM EVEN WHEN I'M
SURROUNDED BY CHAOS.

I WILL LAUGH EVERYDAY, EVEN ON THE ONES
FILLED WITH SADNESS.

IF I NEED HELP, I WILL ASK FOR IT WITHOUT
SHAME.

I AM A POSITIVE ROLE MODEL IN MY CHILDREN'S
LIFE.

I WILL NOT ALLOW OTHER PEOPLE'S CHOICES TO
AFFECT MY LIFE.

I AM UNIQUE, THERE IS NO REASON TO COMPARE
MYSELF TO OTHERS.

I DESERVE TO TAKE A BREAK WHENEVER I NEED
ONE.

I WILL LOOK FOR MORE JOY IN THE SIMPLE
THINGS LIFE HAS TO OFFER.

I AM ALLOWED TO MAKE ROOM IN MY LIFE, SO
THAT THERE WILL BE SPACE FOR GREATER
THINGS.

I WILL SET HEALTHY BOUNDARIES, AND HONOR
THEM.

I WILL BE BRAVE ENOUGH TO ACCEPT
OPPORTUNITIES WHEN THEY ARE PRESENTED TO
ME.

I WILL NOT ALLOW OTHERS' NEGATIVITY TO
AFFECT MY SELF-WORTH.

MY CREATIVITY IS CAPABLE OF LEADING TO
GREAT IDEAS.

I AM GRATEFUL FOR EVERY MOMENT I HAVE
WITH MY CHILDREN.

I AM GRATEFUL FOR EVERY MOMENT I HAVE
WITH MY PARENTS.

I WILL STRIVE TO TRULY LISTEN BEFORE I SPEAK.

I WILL EDUCATE MYSELF ON A TOPIC BEFORE I FORM AN OPINION.

I WILL LOVE MYSELF, FOR EXACTLY WHO I AM, I WILL BE COMFORTABLE IN MY OWN SKIN.

I AM DOING THE BEST I CAN IN EVERYTHING THAT I DO.

I WILL HANDLE EVERY SITUATION WITH COURAGE.

I WILL BE AS GENEROUS AS MY BUDGET ALLOWS.

I WILL NOT BE PRIDEFUL, AND ACCEPT OTHERS' GENEROSITY WHEN I NEED TO.

THE UNIVERSE DOES NOT HAVE A LIMIT ON WHAT I CAN ACCOMPLISH.

I WILL STRIVE TO DO WHAT IS RIGHT, REGARDLESS OF THE CONSEQUENCES.

I WILL TRUST AND FOLLOW MY INTUITION ABOVE ALL ELSE.

I WILL VIEW OBSTACLES AS OPPORTUNITIES FOR GROWTH.

I ALONE AM RESPONSIBLE FOR THE OUTCOMES IN MY LIFE.

I WILL LEARN FROM MY HISTORY AND CHOOSE NOT TO REPEAT MY PAST MISTAKES.

I WILL STRIVE TO STAY HUMBLE, EVEN WHEN I ACHIEVE SUCCESS.

MY FUTURE IS WORTH THE WAIT.

I WILL BE GRATEFUL FOR MY BODY AND MY HEALTH.

MY HEALTH IS A PRIORITY I WILL NOT IGNORE.

IT IS OKAY FOR ME TO ASK FOR MY NEEDS TO BE MET.

I WILL TRUST AND FOLLOW MY INTUITION ABOVE ALL ELSE.

I WILL VIEW OBSTACLES AS OPPORTUNITIES FOR GROWTH.

I ALONE AM RESPONSIBLE FOR THE OUTCOMES IN MY LIFE.

I WILL LEARN FROM MY HISTORY AND CHOOSE NOT TO REPEAT MY PAST MISTAKES.

I WILL STRIVE TO STAY HUMBLE, EVEN WHEN I ACHIEVE SUCCESS.

MY FUTURE IS WORTH THE WAIT.

I WILL BE GRATEFUL FOR MY BODY AND MY HEALTH.

MY HEALTH IS A PRIORITY I WILL NOT IGNORE.

IT IS OKAY FOR ME TO ASK FOR MY NEEDS TO BE MET.

I DO NOT NEED OUTSIDE VALIDATION IN ORDER TO FEEL SUCCESSFUL.

THE UNIVERSE DOES NOT WANT TO SEE ME FAIL.

I DO NOT NEED MAKEUP, I AM BEAUTIFUL IN MY NATURAL STATE.

MY HAIR IS BEAUTIFUL IN ITS NATURAL STATE, AND I WILL EMBRACE IT.

MY SKIN IS BEAUTIFUL DESPITE MY BLEMISHES.

I WILL OPENLY AND TRUTHFULLY COMMUNICATE MY NEEDS.

I WILL RESPECT OTHERS, SO THAT THEY WILL RESPECT ME.

I AM CAPABLE OF COMMUNICATING MY THOUGHTS CLEARLY.

THE MISTREATMENT I RECEIVED AS A CHILD IS NOT MY FAULT.

I WILL NOT CARRY THE BURDEN OF OTHERS.

I WILL NOT CARRY THE BURDEN OF OTHERS.

I FORGIVE MY PARENTS FOR THEIR MISTAKES.

I WILL GUIDE MY CHILDREN THROUGH THEIR MISTAKES.

I WILL STOP CRITICIZING MYSELF, AND FORGIVE MYSELF FOR THE TIMES I HAVE DONE SO IN THE PAST.

I AM BRAVE ENOUGH TO STAND UP AND BE SEEN.

I AM EXACTLY THE PERSON I WAS MEANT TO BE.

NO ONE COULD BE A BETTER ME.

THERE IS A SOLUTION TO EVERY PROBLEM I FACE.

I AM COURAGEOUS ENOUGH TO STEP OUT OF MY COMFORT ZONE IN ORDER TO ACHIEVE MY GOALS.

I WILL WAKE EACH MORNING READY TO LEARN.

I CAN CHOOSE TO RELEASE MY SADNESS.

I AM CAPABLE ENOUGH TO CHOOSE WHO I TRUST.

I AM LOVABLE.

I AM WHOLE.

I AM COMPLETE.

I AM CAPABLE OF CHANGING MY DIET.

I AM CAPABLE OF EATING HEALTHY.

I AM CAPABLE OF CHANGING MY EXERCISE
HABITS.

I WILL MAKE TIME FOR MYSELF, AND HOLD NO
GUILT FOR IT

I AM CAPABLE OF EMPATHY.

I WILL BE EMPATHETIC TO OTHERS.

I AM MOTIVATED.

I WILL TRY MY BEST TO ALWAYS BE
COOPERATIVE.

I AM A RELIABLE FRIEND.

I AM A RELIABLE PARTNER.

I AM A RELIABLE PARENT.

I AM OBSERVANT.

I WILL START EACH DAY WITH OPTIMISM.

I WILL NOT LET OTHERS DAMPER MY
ENTHUSIASM.

I AM IMAGINATIVE.

I AM TRUSTWORTHY.

I AM DETERMINED TO ACHIEVE MY GOALS.

I WILL BE UNAPOLOGETICALLY PERSISTENT.

I AM SINCERE.

I AM CAPABLE OF PATIENCE.

I AM GENEROUS.

I WILL VIEW OTHERS WITH AN OPEN MIND.

I AM FOCUSED.

I AM ALLOWED TO BE QUIET.

I AM CLEVER.

I AM CAPABLE OF THINKING LOGICALLY.

I AM SKILLFUL.

I AM CAPABLE OF SELF-DISCIPLINE.

I AM RESPONSIBLE.

I WILL TREAT OTHERS FAIRLY, THEREFORE I WILL BE TREATED FAIRLY.

I WILL START EACH DAY WITH A CLEAR-HEAD.

I AM CONSIDERATE OF OTHERS AND THEIR FEELINGS.

I WILL NOT ALLOW MYSELF TO BE AFFECTED BY SOMEONE ELSE'S ARGUMENT.

I AM MATURE.

I WILL HOLD MYSELF ACCOUNTABLE FOR MY ACTIONS.

I WILL HOLD MYSELF ACCOUNTABLE FOR MY WORDS.

I AM FULL OF COMPASSION.

I AM A LOYAL PARTNER.

I AM A LOYAL FRIEND.

I AM A TRUSTWORTHY FRIEND.

I AM A TRUSTWORTHY PARTNER.

I AM OBSERVANT.

I WILL STRIVE NOT TO BE BIASED IN ANY ASPECT OF MY LIFE.

I WILL NOT BE CRITICAL OF MYSELF OR MY LOVED ONES.

I AM NOT NEGLECTFUL.

I FORGIVE MY PARENTS FOR THEIR NEGLECT OF ME.

I AM NOT WEAK.

I AM NOT RUDE.

I WILL NOT BE RECKLESS.

MY SHYNESS IS NOT A SIGN OF WEAKNESS.

I WILL BE COURTEOUS TO THOSE AROUND ME, SO THAT THEY ARE COURTEOUS TO ME.

I AM FAITHFUL.

I AM JOYFUL.

I WILL NOT ALLOW ANYONE TO STEAL MY JOY.

I AM AN INTERESTING INDIVIDUAL.

I AM RESOURCEFUL.

I AM THOUGHTFUL.

I AM WITTY.

I WILL BE PERSISTENT IN ACCOMPLISHING MY GOALS.

I AM CONFIDENT.

I WILL NOT LET OTHERS' JUDGEMENT AFFECT MY CONFIDENCE.

I AM FRIENDLY.

I AM A FUN PERSON.

I AM FUNNY.

I AM BOLD, AND I WILL NOT APOLOGIZE FOR IT.

I am affectionate, and capable of accepting affection from others.

I deserve to be safe.

I deserve to be healthy.

I can handle my negative feelings, and push through them.

I am not crazy, and will not allow others to call me so.

I am a survivor.

I deserve to feel better than I do today

I can fight through my depression.

I will not let depression rule my life.

I am not alone.

The situation I am in will not last forever.

I will learn to cope with my fears

BAD FEELINGS ARE TEMPORARY.

I WILL NOT LET MY ANXIETIES CONTROL ME.

IT'S OKAY IF I FEEL ANXIOUS SOMETIMES.

IT'S OKAY IF I FEEL FEAR SOMETIMES.

IT'S OKAY IF I FEEL SAD SOMEDAY.

NOT EVERYTHING HAPPENS FOR A REASON, AND I
ACCEPT THAT.

EVEN THE BEST THINGS COME TO AN END,
EMBRACE IT.

I DESERVE WEALTH.

I AM A LEADER.

I CHOSE TO SEE THE BEAUTY IN THIS WORLD.

I WILL IGNORE HATE.

I WILL IGNORE HATEFUL COMMENTS MADE
ABOUT ME.

IF SOMEONE IS HATEFUL TOWARDS ME, I WILL
RESPOND WITH LOVE.

I CHOOSE TO BELIEVE THERE IS AN OPPORTUNITY INSIDE EVERY EXPERIENCE, EVERY DAY.

I WILL MAKE A DIFFERENCE IN MY LIFE.

I WILL MAKE A DIFFERENCE IN THIS WORLD.

I DESERVE THE BEST OPPORTUNITIES.

I DESERVE TO BE PAID THE SAME AMOUNT AS OTHERS IN MY INDUSTRY, REGARDLESS OF GENDER.

MY OPINIONS MATTER, AND SHOULD BE HEARD.

MY FEELINGS MATTER AND SHOULD BE HEARD.

MY FEARS ARE VALID, EVEN IF THEY ARE UNJUSTIFIED.

I BELIEVE THAT MY CHILDREN LOVE AND SUPPORT ME.

I LOVE AND SUPPORT MY CHILDREN.

I HOLD THE POWER TO CHANGE THE WORLD IF I SO CHOOSE.

I EMBRACE MY CURLY, AND KNOW IT'S BEAUTIFUL.

I AM AN INTEGRAL MEMBER OF MY FAMILY.

I AM CAPABLE OF SMART DECISIONS.

I AM MATURE, AND WILL NOT STOOP TO THE LENGTHS OF OTHERS.

I AM LOVED BY OTHERS.

I AM LIKED BY OTHERS.

MY FAMILY LOVES ME FOR ME.

MY CHILDREN LOVE ME UNCONDITIONALLY.

MY HUSBAND LOVES ME UNCONDITIONALLY.

MY WIFE LOVES ME UNCONDITIONALLY.

MY PARTNER LOVES ME UNCONDITIONALLY.

I AM PROUD OF MY HERITAGE.

I AM PROUD OF MY LINEAGE.

I AM PROUD OF MY FAITH.

I AM PROUD OF THE COLOR OF MY SKIN.

THE COLOR OF MY SKIN IS BEAUTIFUL.

THE TEXTURE OF MY HAIR IS BEAUTIFUL.

I AM PROUD OF MY TEXTURED HAIR.

I AM HARDWORKING.

MY DISABILITY DOES NOT DEFINE WHO I AM.

I AM INTELLIGENT DESPITE MY DISABILITIES.

I WILL NOT ALLOW MY DISABILITIES TO HOLD ME BACK.

I DESERVE TO BE LOVED AND RESPECTED.

I DESERVE AN HONEST PARTNER.

I AM MENTALLY STRONG.

I AM PHYSICALLY STRONG.

I AM PHYSICALLY CAPABLE.

I AM MENTALLY CAPABLE.

I AM AN ASSET.

I AM AN ASSET TO MY COMPANY.

I AM VALUABLE TO MY FAMILY.

I AM VALUABLE TO MY FRIENDS.

I AM VALUABLE TO THIS WORLD.

I AM UNIQUE.

I AM A SURVIVOR.

I AM PASSIONATE.

MY MIND IS POWERFUL.

I AM POWERFUL.

I AM CONSTANTLY EVOLVING, AND I WILL NOT APOLOGIZE FOR IT.

I AM A GIVING PERSON.

TODAY I WILL TAKE THE FIRST STEP TO CHANGE MY LIFE.

I WILL KEEP MOVING FORWARD EVEN IF IT'S ONLY ONE STEP AT A TIME.

I WILL HAVE NO SHAME FOR THE PACE IN WHICH MY LIFE MOVES.

I AM SEXY.

I AM ATTRACTIVE.

I DO NOT NEED TO BE IN A RELATIONSHIP TO FEEL WHOLE.

MY STORY IS INSPIRING.

I AM INSPIRING.

I HAVE A STORY TO TELL THE WORLD, MY STORY.

I WILL NOT STOP UNTIL I ACCOMPLISH MY DREAMS.

MY BODY IS DIVINE.

MY SOUL IS PURE.

MY HEART IS PURE.

MY INTENTIONS ARE GOOD.

I DO NOT HAVE TO PROVE MY WORTH TO ANYONE.

My true self is better than who others think I should be.

I choose to always empower myself and those around me.

I will accept others for exactly who they are.

I will take whatever steps I need to in order to safeguard my peace and happiness.

I approve of me.

I am determined to do amazing things in this lifetime.

I will make the most of life, even when it's not easy.

I will start the morning with Grace.

My children do not need a perfect mother, they need me.

I AM A GOOD PROVIDER FOR MY FAMILY.

I AM MY CHILDREN'S HOME.

I AM MY CHILDREN'S SAFE PLACE.

I DO NOT NEED AN EXPENSIVE CAR, ONLY ONE THAT IS RELIABLE.

I WILL TRUST IN MY GOD.

I VALUE SINCERITY.

I AM A SINCERE PERSON.

I WILL NOT AVOID THE MIRROR, I WILL LEARN TO LOVE THE REFLECTION STARING BACK AT ME.

I WILL NOT LIVE IN FEAR OF DEATH.

I WILL PRIORITIZE MY HEALTH.

I WILL PRIORITIZE MY HAPPINESS.

I WILL PRIORITIZE MY CHILDREN'S HAPPINESS.

I WILL PRIORITIZE MY FAMILY'S HAPPINESS.

I DESERVE COMFORT.

I DESERVE SECOND CHANCES.

I WILL BE BRAVE ENOUGH TO OFFER SECOND
CHANCES.

I WILL BE COURAGEOUS ENOUGH TO FORGIVE.

I AM BOTH LOVEABLE AND LOVING.

I AM WORTHY AND VALUABLE.

I AM FABULOUS.

I DESERVE A PROSPEROUS LIFE.

I WILL NO LONGER CARRY THE BURDEN OF LOW
SELF-ESTEEM.

I WILL NO LONGER CARRY THE BURDEN OF GUILT,
I FORGIVE MYSELF.

I WILL NO LONGER CARRY THE BURDEN OF
SELF-DOUBT.

I WILL NOT APOLOGIZE FOR MY CONFIDENCE.

I AM ONE IN EIGHT BILLION.

I AM OPEN AND WILLING TO RECEIVE LOVE.

I AM OPEN AND WILLING TO RECEIVE COMPLIMENTS.

I AM CAPABLE OF BUILDING WEALTH.

I DESERVE TO BECOME WEALTHY.

I AM AN UNDERSTANDING INDIVIDUAL, AND IN RETURN DESERVE TO BE UNDERSTOOD.

I WILL NOT APOLOGIZE FOR THE HEALTHY HOBBIES I ENJOY.

I WILL NOT APOLOGIZE FOR IMPOSING HEALTHY EATING HABITS ON MYSELF AND MY CHILDREN.

I WILL NOT APOLOGIZE FOR MY ENERGY LEVEL.

SOME DAYS I WILL MAKE BAD DECISIONS, THAT DOES NOT MAKE ME A BAD PERSON.

I DESERVE TO HAVE THE CAREER OF MY DREAMS.

I WILL NOT APOLOGIZE FOR BEING TIRED.

I DESERVE REST AND RELAXATION.

I DESERVE SLEEP.

I AM A POWERFUL INDIVIDUAL.

I WILL ALWAYS CHOOSE MY SIDE.

I AM ALLOWED TO SPLURGE ON MYSELF.

I AM ALLOWED A BREAK FROM MY CHILDREN,
AND THAT DOES NOT MAKE ME A BAD MOM.

I DESERVE A BREAK FROM MY HUSBAND, AND
THAT DOES NOT MAKE ME A BAD WIFE.

I DESERVE A BREAK FROM MY WIFE, AND THAT
DOES NOT MAKE ME A BAD WIFE.

I DESERVE A BREAK FROM MY PARTNER, AND
THAT DOES NOT MAKE ME A BAD PARTNER.

I DESERVE ALONE TIME.

I DESERVE TIME FOR MYSELF.

I DESERVE FRIENDS.

I RADIATE POSITIVITY.

I RADIATE GOOD VIBES.

I RADIATE LOVE.

I RADIATE KINDNESS.

I AM ADORED BY MY FRIENDS.

I AM ADORED BY MY CHILDREN.

I AM ADORED BY MY HUSBAND.

I AM ADORED BY MY WIFE.

I AM ADORED BY MY PARTNER.

I AM SUPPORTED.

I WILL NOT BE ASHAMED TO ASK MY PARENTS FOR HELP.

I WILL NOT BE ASHAMED TO ASK MY BOSS FOR HELP, IT'S NOT POSSIBLE TO KNOW EVERYTHING.

I AM UNSTOPPABLE.

I AM A CHERISHED MEMBER OF SOCIETY.

I HAVE SOMETHING OF VALUE TO ADD TO THIS WORLD.

I DESERVE SOMEONE'S BEST.

I WILL NOT ALLOW ANYONE TO MAKE ME FEEL INFERIOR.

ONLY I GET TO DECIDE IF I'M GOOD ENOUGH OR NOT.

I AM UNAPOLOGETICALLY FIERCE.

I AM UNAPOLOGETICALLY FEARLESS.

EVERY SINGLE DAY MAKES ME STRONGER.

I REFUSE TO HOLD HATE IN MY HEART.

I WILL NOT GO TO BED WITH UNRESOLVED FAMILIAL ISSUES.

I'M ALLOWED TO LEAVE ANY SITUATION WHEN I FEEL UNCOMFORTABLE.

I WILL TRUST MY INSTINCTS ABOVE
EVERYTHING.

I AM WORTHY OF VALIDATION.

I UNDERSTAND THAT CHANGE TAKES TIME.

I AM UNAPOLOGETICALLY CONFIDENT IN MY
ABILITIES.

I WILL EXCEL IN THIS LIFE.

MY DREAMS ARE READY FOR ME NOW, ALL I
HAVE TO DO IS GRAB THEM.

MY DETERMINATION IS UNPARALLELED.

I AM BRAVE ENOUGH TO SUCCEED.

THERE IS SOMETHING FOR ME TO LEARN EVERY
SINGLE DAY.

TOMORROW I WILL DO BETTER.

I WILL BE GRATEFUL FOR THE BLESSINGS EACH
DAY BRINGS.

I AM GRATEFUL FOR THE BODY I HAVE.

I AM GRATEFUL FOR MY SPOUSE.

MY GOALS ARE ALLOWED TO BE BIG, THEY ARE MINE TO REACH.

I DESERVE INNER PEACE.

I WILL ADMIRE THE BEAUTY OF NATURE EVERY DAY.

I WILL PRACTICE TOLERANCE.

I CHOOSE NOT TO BE TRAPPED IN THE PAST.

I CHOOSE TO LIVE IN THE PRESENT.

I CHOOSE TO BE HOPEFUL ABOUT MY FUTURE.

I REFUSE TO BE HELD BACK BECAUSE OF THE TRAUMAS I HAVE ENDURED.

I AM STRONGER THAN MY TRAUMA.

MY PAST TRAUMA HAS NO HOLD ON WHO I AM TODAY.

My past trauma does not define my future.

I am strong enough to heal from childhood.

I am strong enough to cut people out of my life who do not value me.

My worth is not defined by you.

I free myself from negativity.

I free myself from toxic people.

I free myself from toxic situations.

I free myself from those who have chosen to hurt me.

I will treat myself as though I am my own best friend.

My secrets are mine to keep.

Other than my children, I do not owe anyone anything.

I WILL NOT ALLOW NEGATIVE COMMENTS ABOUT MY WEIGHT AFFECT ME.

NO ONE KNOWS ME BETTER THAN ME.

I AM HUMAN, I MAKE MISTAKES, AND I FORGIVE MYSELF FOR THEM.

I WILL LOOK AT EVERY OPPORTUNITY AS ONE TO LEARN.

SOMETIMES YOU JUST HAVE TO LOOK IN THE MIRROR AND TELL YOUR INNER VOICE TO SHUT UP.

GO OUTSIDE, SCREAM, I PROMISE YOU WILL FEEL BETTER.

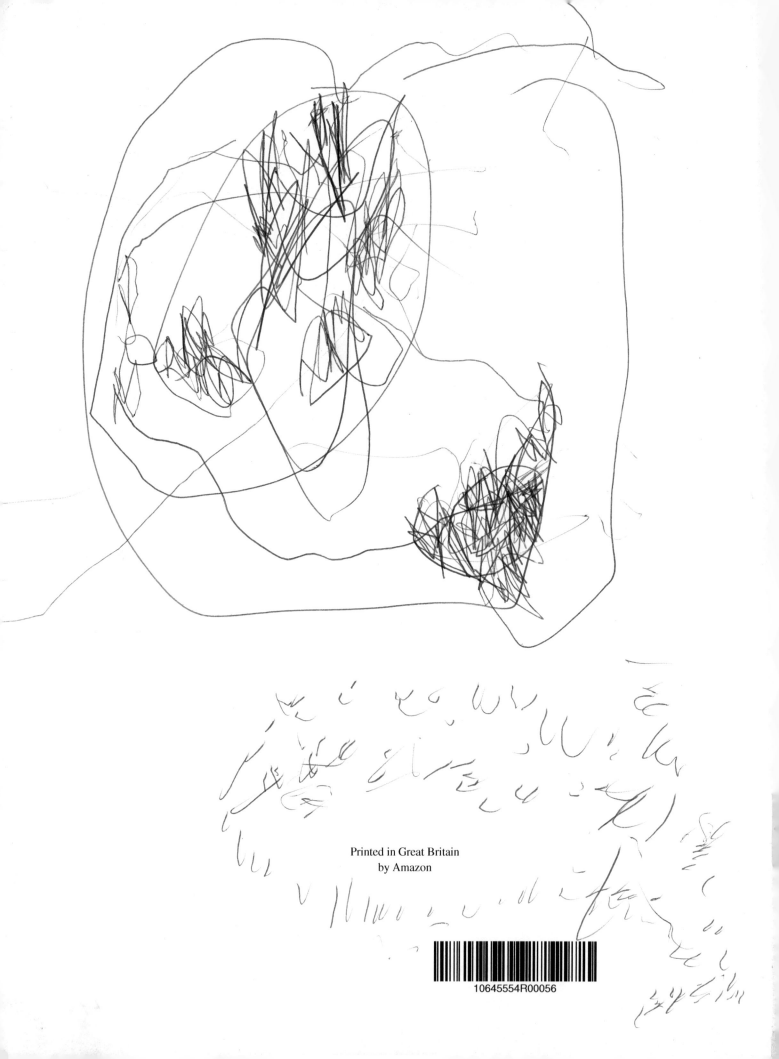

Printed in Great Britain
by Amazon